# Beginning Sounds

Say the word for each picture.
Write the **beginning** sound.
Use these letters: **c, f, h, k, m, p, r, t.**

1.

an

2.

ie

3.

ain

4.

at

5.

at

6.

an

7.

ie

8.

ite

# Beginning Sounds

Say the word for each picture.
Write the **beginning** sound.
Use these letters: **b, d, g, l, n, q, s, y**.

1. eaf

2. og

3. all

4. ueen

5. arn

6. oat

7. ine

8. oap

# Ending Sounds

Say the word for each picture.
Write the **ending** sound.
Use these letters: **b, g, l, m, n, p, r, x.**

1.

pi _____

2.

su _____

3.

cu _____

4.

tu _____

5.

nai _____

6.

fo _____

7.

bea _____

8.

dru _____

# Ending Sounds

Say the word for each picture.
Write the **ending** sound.
Use these letters: **d, f, k, l, o, s, t, r.**

1. be____

2. sea____

3. ca____

4. e____l

5. o____

6. bu____

7. ca____

8. boo____

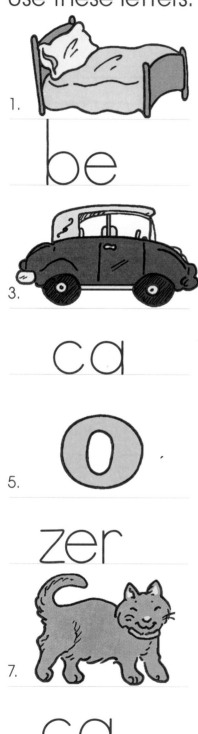

# Review

Say the word for each picture.
Write the **beginning** and **ending** sounds.
Use these letters: **m, n, p, s, g, t, b**.

1.

a

2.

o

3.

e

4.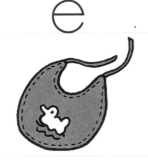

u

5.

i

6.

a

7.

u

8.

e

# Words with Short a

These words have the short **a** sound in .
Say the words.

| pan | map | fan |
|-----|-----|-----|
| nap | dad | bat |

Write two words that **rhyme** with each picture.

1. _____

_____

_____

2. _____

_____

_____

Write the word that **begins** with the same letter as each picture.

1. _____

2. _____

# Words with Short a

Write the short **a** words.
Then color the short **a** words in the picture blue.

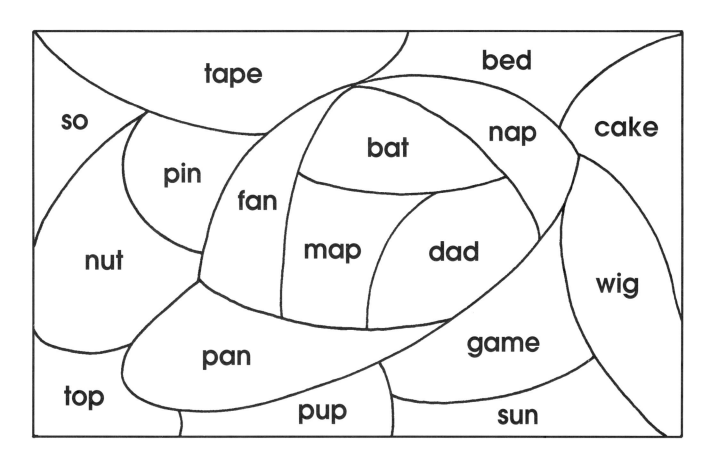

# Words with Short e

These words have the short **e** sound in .
Say the words.

| pen | ten | bell |
|-----|-----|------|
| net | pet | bed |

Write the word that fits each shape.

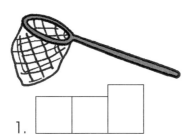

1. ⬚⬚⬚

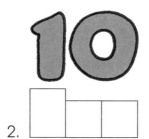

2. ⬚⬚⬚

3. ⬚⬚⬚

4. ⬚⬚⬚

Write the word for each picture.

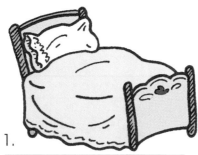

1. _____

2. _____

# Words with Short e

Write the short **e** words.
Then color the short **e** words in the picture red.

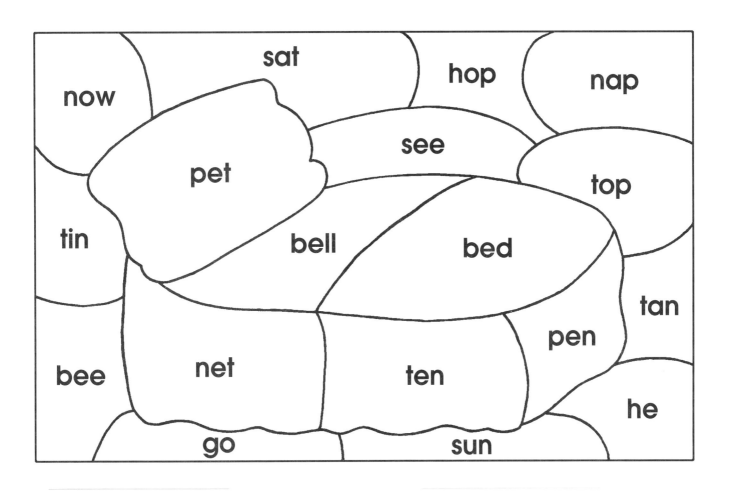

# Words with Short i

These words have the short **i** sound in .
Say the words.

| | | |
|---|---|---|
| **big** | **dig** | **in** |
| **pig** | **wig** | **his** |

Write a word that means the **opposite** of:

1.  out

2.  hers

Write the words **ending** with **-ig**.

# Words with Short i

Write the short **i** words.
Then color the short **i** words in the picture pink.

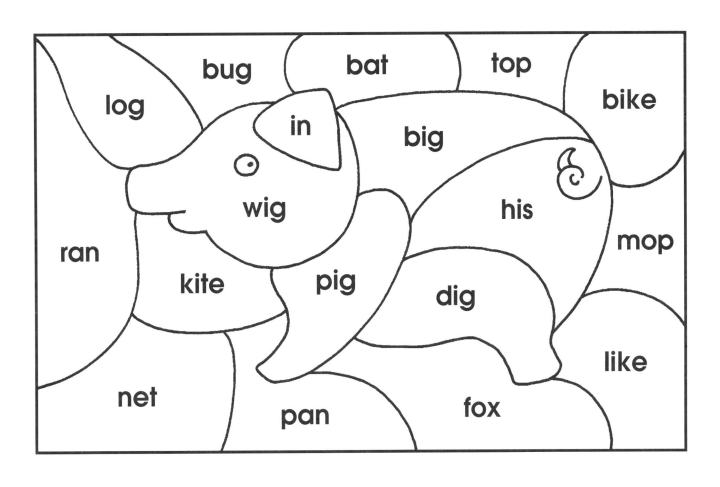

# Words with Short o

These words have the short **o** sound in .
Say the words.

| | | |
|---|---|---|
| top | box | sock |
| pot | not | lot |

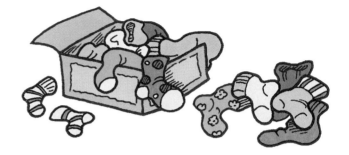

Write the word for each picture inside the shape.

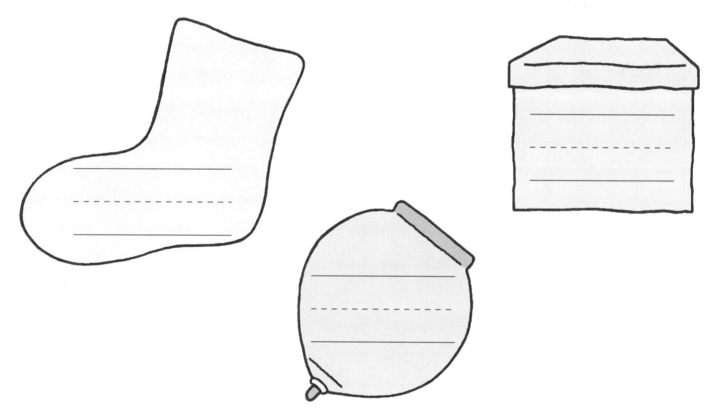

Write the words that **rhyme** with **hot**.

# Words with Short o

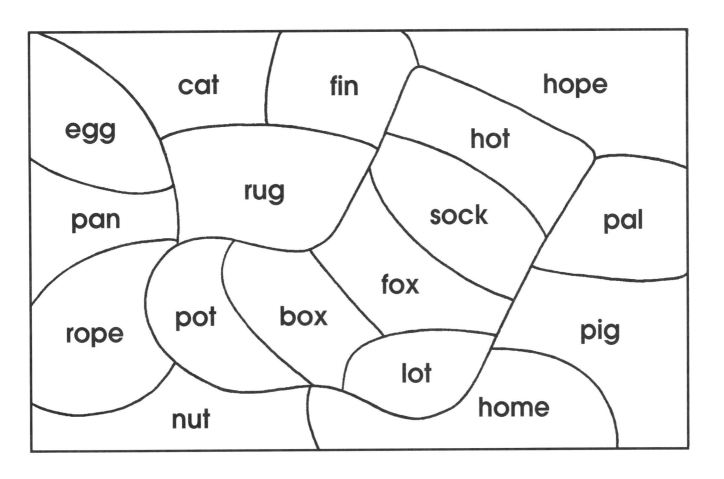

Write the short **o** words.
Then color the short **o** words in the picture orange.

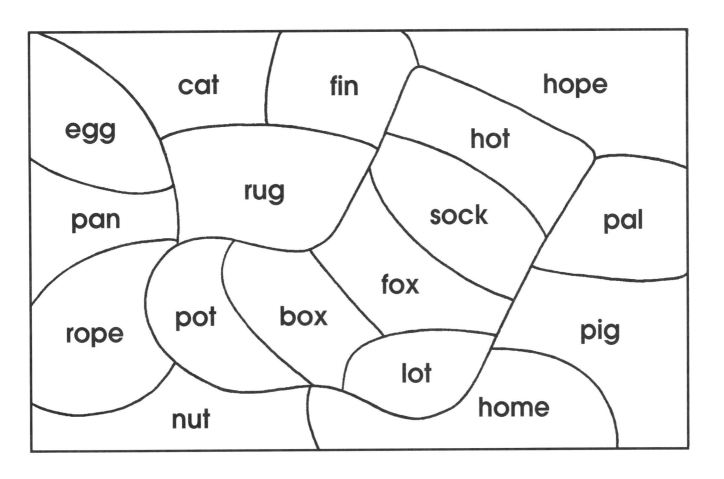

cat

fin

hope

egg

hot

rug

sock

pan

pal

fox

rope

pot

box

pig

lot

nut

home

# Words with Short u

These words have the short **u** sound in .
Say the words.

| | | |
|---|---|---|
| sun | rug | us |
| hug | up | run |

Write a word that means the opposite of:

1.  down  _____

2.  moon  _____

3.  walk  _____

Write another word that begins with the same letter as each picture.

1. _____

2. _____

3. _____

# Words with Short u

Write the short **u** word for each picture.
Say the words.

| | | |
|---|---|---|
| up | sun | rug |
| run | hug | bus |

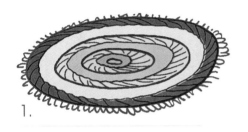

1. _____

2. _____

3. _____

4. _____

5. _____

6. _____

# Review

Say the word for each picture.
Write the vowel.
Use these letters: **a, e, i, o, u.**

1.

b ___ ll

2.

b ___ b

3.

r ___ g

4.

b ___ t

5.

b ___ x

6.

v ___ n

7.

b ___ s

8.

w ___ b

# Words with Long a

These words have the long **a** sound in .
Say the words.

| | | |
|---|---|---|
| rake | game | tape |
| vase | cake | gate |

Write the answers on the lines.

1. You can put  in me.
   What am I? _____

2. You like to eat me.
   What am I? _____

3. I fix a torn page.
   What am I? _____

4. You use me to pile  .
   What am I? _____

Write the words with the same **beginning** sound as  .

_____          _____

# Words with Long a

Write the long **a** word for each picture.
Say the words.

| tape | rake | cake |
|------|------|------|
| game | vase | gate |

1. _____

2. _____

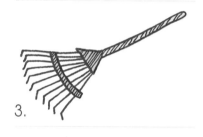

3. _____

4. _____

5. _____

6. _____

# Words with Long e

These words have the long **e** sound in .
Say the words.

| | | |
|---|---|---|
| he | me | see |
| three | tree | she |

Write two 2-letter words that rhyme with **bee**.

Write two 3-letter words that rhyme with **bee**.

Write the word for each picture.

1.

2. **3**

# Words with Long e

Write the long **e** words.
Then color the long **e** words in the picture green.

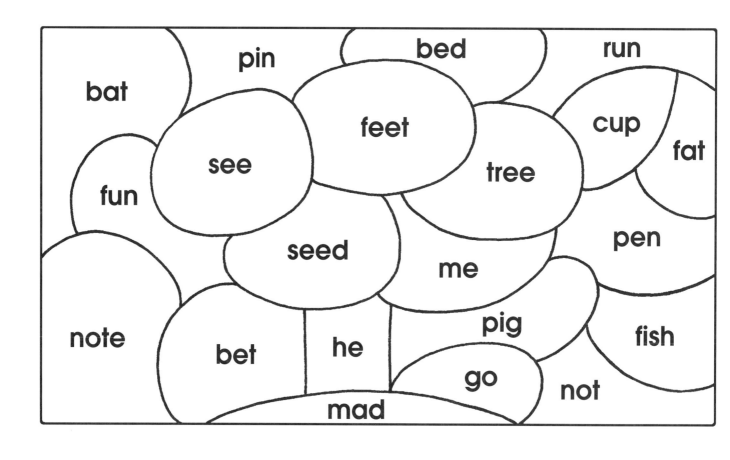

# Words with Long i

These words have the long **i** sound in .
Say the words.

| | | |
|---|---|---|
| kite | tie | fine |
| bike | like | ride |

Write the answers on the lines.

1. You can fly me.
   What am I?

2. You can ride me.
   What am I?

3. I am something to wear.
   What am I?

Write the three other words that fit these shapes.

1. ⬜⬜⬜⬜    2. ⬜⬜⬜⬜    3. ⬜⬜⬜⬜

# Words with Long i

Write the long **i** words.
Then color the long **i** words in the picture purple.

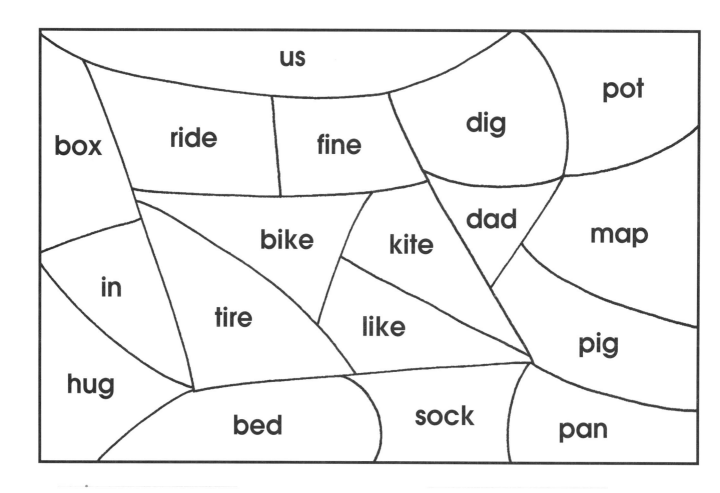

These words have the long **o** sound in .
Say the words.

home    nose    joke
gold    fold    note

e h j k m n o s t
△ ⊖ ☆ ◇ < > ○ □ ▯

Use the code to write the words.
Write the letter each shape shows.

 > ○ ▯ △

 ⊖ ○ < △

1.

☆ ○ ◇ △

2.

> ○ □ △

3.

4.

Write the words that **rhyme** with **told**.

# Words with Long o

Write the long **o** words.
Then color the long **o** words in the picture blue.

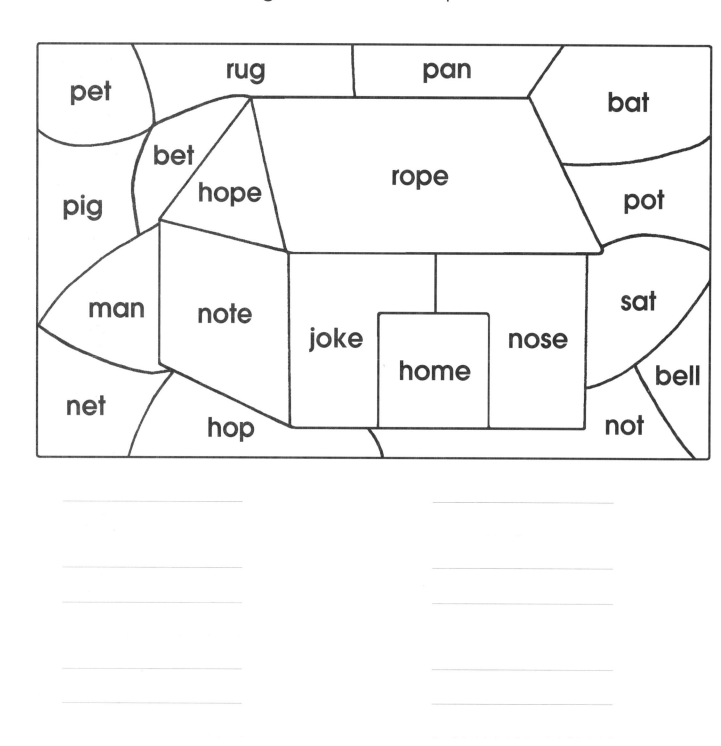

_____    _____

_____    _____

_____    _____

_____    _____

# Words with Long u

These words have the long **u** sound in .
Say the words.

| | | |
|---|---|---|
| cube | cute | huge |
| rule | mule | tube |

c  e  g  h  l  r  t  u  b
△  ⬭  ☆  ◇  <  >  ○  □  ▯

Use the code to write the words.
Write the letter each shape shows.

△ □ ○ ⬭ _____

○ □ ▯ ⬭ _____

1.

◇ □ ☆ ⬭ _____

> □ < ⬭ _____

3.

2.

4.

Write the word for each picture.

1. _____

2. _____

# Words with Long u

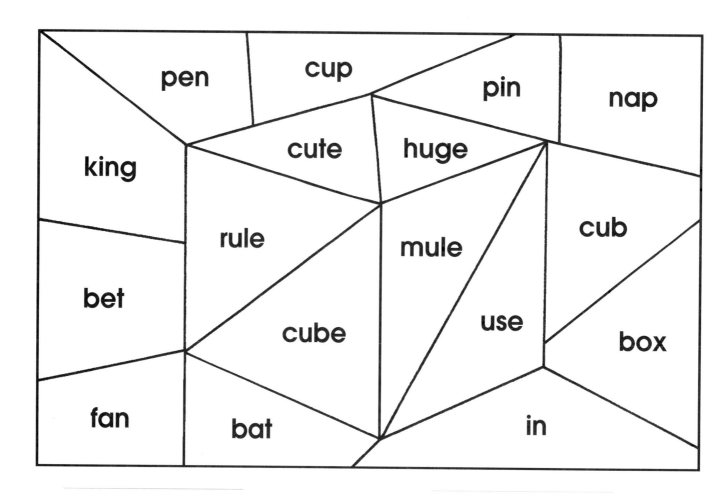

Write the long **u** words.
Then color the long **u** words in the picture red.

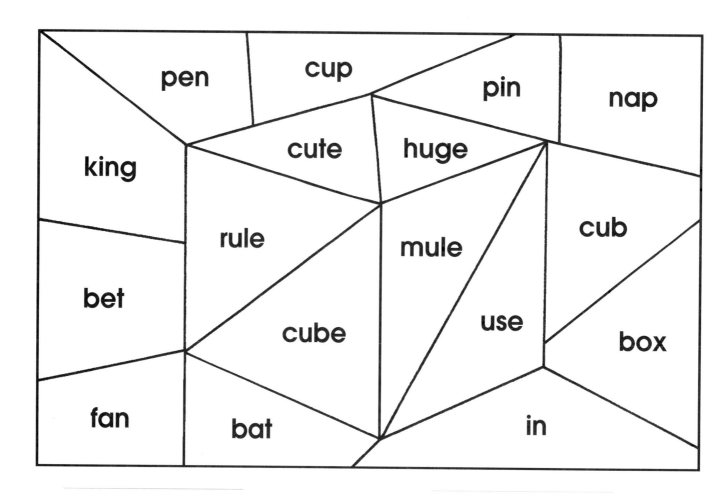

pen

cup

pin

nap

king

cute

huge

cub

rule

mule

bet

cube

use

box

fan

bat

in

# Review

Write the short **a** word in each blank.

nap   maps
bat   Dad

Sam walks to school.

He learns about _____ .

At recess he plays with a ball and _____ .

_____ drives him home.

Sam is tired so he takes a _____ .

Circle all the short **e** words.

| tent | bed | let | net |
|------|-----|-----|-----|
| see  | pen | she | key |

# Review

Write the answers on the lines.

> fox    sock    box    pot

1. You put me on your foot.
   What am I? _____

2. I hold toys for you.
   What am I? _____

3. Mom uses me to cook.
   What am I? _____

4. I am an animal.
   What am I? _____

a b c d e f g h i j k l m n o p q r s t u v w x y z
Write the words in alphabetical order.

> us    hug    sun

1. _____    2. _____    3. _____

# Review

Write the **a** word in each blank.

> game    rake
> vase    gate

Bring a _____ to pile the leaves.

We will pick flowers to put in a _____.

Then we can play a _____ of tag.

Don't go past the _____.

Circle all the long **e** words.

**net**          **tree**          **he**          **seed**

**see**          **get**          **ten**          **bee**

# Review

Write the answers on the lines.

| nose | rope | note | home |
|------|------|------|------|

1. You can tie things with me.
   What am I?

2. You use me to smell.
   What am I?

3. You live in me.
   What am I?

4. You write me.
   What am I?

a b c d e f g h i j k l m n o p q r s t u v w x y z
Write the words in alphabetical order.

| mule | rule | cute |
|------|------|------|

1.                    2.                    3.

# Review

Write five sentences using one of these words in each sentence.

> game     home     in
> like     Dad

1.

2.

3.

4.

5.

# Answer Key

**Page 1**
1. fan   2. pie
3. rain   4. cat
5. hat   6. man
7. tie   8. kite

**Page 2**
1. leaf   2. dog
3. ball   4. queen
5. yarn   6. goat
7. nine   8. soap

**Page 3**
1. pig   2. sun
3. cup   4. tub
5. nail   6. fox
7. bear   8. drum

**Page 4**
1. bed   2. seal
3. car   4. elf
5. zero   6. bus
7. cat   8. book

**Page 5**
1. man   2. mop
3. pen   4. sun
5. bib   6. pan
7. bug   8. ten

**Page 6**
1. pan   2. map
   fan      nap

1. dad   2. bat

**Page 7**
fan, map,
pan, bat,
dad, nap

**Page 8**
1. net   2. ten
3. pen   4. pet

1. bed   2. bell

**Page 9**
pet, pen, ten,
bed, bell, net

**Page 10**
1. in
2. his

big, pig,
dig, wig

**Page 11**
in, his, wig,
big, pig, dig

**Page 12**
sock, top, box

pot, not, lot

**Page 13**
box, hot, sock,
fox, pot, lot

**Page 14**
1. up
2. sun
3. run

1. hug   2. rug   3. us

**Page 15**
1. rug   2. up
3. sun   4. hug
5. bus   6. run

**Page 16**
1. bell   2. bib
3. rug   4. bat
5. box   6. van
7. bus   8. web

**Page 17**
1. vase
2. cake
3. tape
4. rake

game, gate

**Page 18**
1. vase   2. gate
3. rake   4. cake
5. tape   6. game

**Page 19**
he, me

see, she

1. tree   2. three

**Page 20**
see, feet,
me, tree,
he, seed

**Page 21**
1. kite
2. bike
3. tie

1. ride   2. fine   3. like

**Page 22**
kite, ride,
fine, tire,
bike, like

**Page 23**
1. note   2. home
3. joke   4. nose

fold, gold

**Page 24**
nose, rope,
home, note,
hope, joke

**Page 25**
1. cute   2. tube
3. huge   4. rule

1. mule   2. cube

**Page 26**
cube, use,
rule, huge,
cute, mule

**Page 27**
Sam walks to school.
He learns about **maps**.
At recess he plays with a ball and **bat**.
**Dad** drives him home.
Sam is tired so he takes a **nap**.

tent, bed, pen, let, net

**Page 28**
1. sock
2. box
3. pot
4. fox

1. hug   2. sun   3. us

**Page 29**
Bring a **rake** to pile the leaves.
We will pick flowers to put in a **vase**.
Then we can play a **game** of tag.
Don't go past the **gate**.

see, tree, he, seed, bee

**Page 30**
1. rope
2. nose
3. home
4. note

1. cute   2. mule   3. rule

**Page 31**
Automatic fill-in.